REBUILDING
BROKEN TRUST

Rebuilding Broken Trust

Help For Those With Honest Doubts

–a transcript & study guide–

Erwin W. Lutzer

Moody Church Media
Chicago

Unless otherwise indicated, all Scripture quotations are taken from *The Holy Bible,* English Standard Version. ESV® Text Edition: 2016. Copyright © 2001 by Crossway Bibles, a publishing ministry of Good News Publishers.

Cover by Bryan Butler

REBUILDING BROKEN TRUST
Copyright © 2023 by Erwin W. Lutzer
Published by Moody Church Media
Chicago, Illinois 60614
www.moodymedia.org

ISBN: 9798857785645

A transcript of the message,
"Rebuilding Broken Trust" on Psalm 73.
Preached at The Moody Church
on August 27, 2023.
This transcript has been edited.

moodymedia.org/rebuilding
Watch or listen to Pastor Lutzer's entire message.

ERWIN W. LUTZER

FOREWORD

This transcript and study guide is intended to facilitate reflection on the message, *Rebuilding Broken Trust: Help For Those With Honest Doubts.* In this message, I observe three mistakes Asaph made during his process of deconstruction. I share personal stories and insights, while offering advice and cautions for those in various stages of deconstruction.

This guide can be used for both individual and group use. Included within are: 1.) the transcript of the message, 2.) the study guide questions, and 3.) a direct link to the audio/video.

It might be helpful to take notes while reading or watching the sermon. Be sure to prepare by making observations and considering how this message applies to your life.

I trust this resource will encourage and equip you to be near God in your honest doubts.

Pastor Lutzer

ERWIN W. LUTZER

REBUILDING BROKEN TRUST

Well, my topic today is rebuilding broken trust. Rebuilding broken trust.

About ten years ago, a new word came into our vocabulary. Now it's been around for a lot longer than that, but the word is "deconstruction." The word deconstruction means exactly as it sounds. When you construct something, you build something; and deconstruction is to take it apart. It's to dismantle it. So, when people today talk about dismantling the Constitution, they mean going behind and trying to see why the church fathers didn't believe what they wrote, and so forth, and oftentimes that's the way deconstruction is defined.

When it comes to the Christian faith, it's on a continuum. There are those who have questions about the Christian faith, and so they're going through a period of doubt, which is very normal. I think all of us went through a period of time in our lives when we needed to wrestle through some issues, have some doubts, until we made our parents' faith our own.

But on the other hand, there are those who, when they deconstruct, they actually not only leave the church, but they leave the Christian faith entirely. The Bible has a word for that, and it is the word "apostatize." In other words, they totally leave the faith.

So, I want to define the word "deconstruction" for our purposes today as a crisis of faith. It may be a serious crisis, it may be a passing crisis, but it is a crisis of faith. And when you look in the Bible, you discover there is a man in the Old Testament who went through a crisis of faith. He almost abandoned faith in God, but he was pulled back from the brink. And then he explains, first of all, why he almost deconstructed, then he tells us what he learned and the mistakes he made. So that's our journey today as we look at Psalm 73.

It is so important for you to look at this in your Bibles. If you have the Bible on your cellphone, look at it there. I know there are Bibles there in the pews, and wherever you can find Psalm 73, take time to find it.

Now, before we get into the text, I want to tell you two things. First, fifty years ago, a professor of mine preached a message on this text, and it was so impactful that when I went to prepare this message, bits and pieces of his outline are reflected in what I have to say today. Now, if you remember a sermon that was preached fifty years ago, you know it was a great sermon. It's not a tribute to my memory. It's a tribute to the effectiveness with which he preached. I don't know that any of you are going to remember this sermon for fifty years, but who knows?

The second thing I want to point out is when I was younger, fifty years ago, I spent a lot of time memorizing huge passages of Scripture, some of the books of the New Testament, and also ten of the Psalms. And one of the Psalms I memorized was Psalm 73, and so if you find me quoting part of it in this message and the words don't exactly line up to your translation, that will be the explanation for that.

With that introduction, we find in verse 1 of Psalm 73, Asaph, who was a musician by the way, he was part of the musicians in the temple. He begins by saying, "Truly God is good to Israel, to those who are pure in heart." What a wonderful statement to begin with. But then he begins to launch into reasons why he had doubted the goodness of God, and why he almost left the faith.

He said, "But as for me, my feet were almost gone; my steps had well nigh slipped," and now he gives three reasons for his doubts. First of all, he says, "I looked around," and what does he say in verse 3? "I was envious of the arrogant when I saw the prosperity of the wicked." And when the word "wicked" is used, it doesn't mean some kind of a gangster. The word wicked, actually, just refers to people living their life without God.

He said, "I became envious of them when I saw their prosperity." Number one, he said, "They are richer, they are wealthier than I am." In fact, later on in the text, he actually says very clearly that they increased in riches.

Now, here's what he's thinking. He's saying, "If God were to run this world correctly, obviously those who trust in God would be better off financially than those who didn't," but he says, "I walked through their crops and I noticed their crop is higher than mine." He said, "I noticed they are driving some of the latest chariots. They have a better chariot than I do." He said, "This doesn't add up, because there are people who trust God who don't know how to pay their bills; they don't know where the next dollar is coming from." So, he says first of all, "They are wealthier than I am," and then he actually says, "They are healthier." Verse 4, "For they have no pangs until death"; "Their strength is firm." He said, "[Their eyes] stand out with fatness." In those days, that was a great compliment because there was a lot of hunger and there were a lot of people who were in starvation, and so the wealthy actually— they were healthier and they seemed to die well.

Rebecca and I know an oncologist who directly or indirectly has presided over thousands of deaths, and to my shock he said, "Sometimes the unconverted actually die better in this regard," he says, "Christians always say to themselves, 'Oh, God is going to heal me, God is going to heal me,' and they live in denial." (And you know denial is not just a river in Egypt.) [*laughter*] So, what they do is, they avoid reality. He said the non-Christians, they say "I'm not expecting God to heal me," and so they die. Some of them die fearfully, some of them not fearfully. So, he says, "They're wealthier than I am, they're healthier, they're more carefree, they are living their life with a sense of pride." He says, "They are not stricken like the rest of mankind."

Verse 6: "Therefore pride is their necklace; violence covers them as a garment. Their eyes swell out through fatness; their hearts overflow with follies. They scoff and speak with malice." He says they speak against the Most High. They curse God. I love the way he describes it as them walking through this earth and they aren't walking, they are strutting. And he says, "They're tongues, they strut, and their tongues are against the heavens."

And they seem to be getting by. As a matter of fact, he says in verse 11, "They say, 'How can God know? Is there knowledge in the Most High?'" "He's not doing anything. We're going to get by with this."

So Asaph is looking at this and saying, "This really doesn't add up, how they can be that way and they appear to be enjoying life. They've got lots of money, and here's me, poor, unable to pay my bills, and going through a very difficult time." He says, "I'm stricken every morning" in the text. Maybe he means he wakes up with a migraine every morning.

So, what is the payoff? What is the R.O.I., the return of the investment? He says finally in verse 13— It's a very sad verse. He says, "Verily I have cleansed my heart in vain, and washed my hands in innocency." It says here, "I've washed my hands in innocence." "[All] in vain have I kept my heart clean."

What's the payoff? I remember speaking to a young woman who said, "I'm a virgin because my body belongs to God. I wanted to honor God in my body," and she said, "All of my friends are sleeping around. They're carousing on the weekends. They're having all of these drinking parties," and she said, "I have to go back to my lonely apartment." So that's what you get for trusting God, right?

Many years ago, I was in another country, and I needed to buy a piece of equipment for my camera. And they sent me to a man. And they said, "He's a Christian. Go to his shop." So, I did. I discovered he was a Christian. I had a talk with him, and he said to me, "I want you to know that I don't run this business honestly because," he said, "if I did, I wouldn't make any money." He said, "Do you see these other shops? They're all cheating. I have to cheat too."

I urged him, I said, "Why don't you just run your business according to God's direction and with integrity and honesty and take the consequences? If your shop goes down, it goes down, but maybe God will have some surprise for you, and maybe He'll bless you in unexpected ways."

I don't know whether or not he took my advice, but the point is, what is the advantage of believing in God and being a Christian? "In vain I've kept my heart pure."

Now as he was struggling with this, he [Asaph] says in verse 14, "For all the day long I have been stricken and rebuked every morning." Verse 16, "But when I thought how to understand this, it seemed to me a wearisome task." (It became so wearisome to me I couldn't make sense of it.) And then he says, finally, "If I would speak thus." (This actually is verse 15.) "If I had said, 'I will speak thus,' I would have betrayed the generation of your children."

Asaph said, "I didn't spread my doubts around to others lest I cause them to stumble." He said, "I didn't go on Facebook and tell everybody, 'I'm deconstructing, and I want everybody else to know I'm deconstructing and I'm leaving the Christian faith," and, "Why don't you leave with me?'"

Asaph said, "I didn't want to betray the generation. I kept this to myself. I worked through it." Of course, others helped him because he went into the temple of God, but he said, "I struggled with this, and I didn't do any damage in the life of anyone else." And then he tells us, finally in verse 17: "Until I went into the sanctuary of God; then I discerned their end." He said, "When I went into the temple of God, I was totally reoriented." He said, "I saw life from an entirely different point of view, and this point of view helped me to look at life on the long range and I saw their end." And he said, "That's what kept me from deconstructing."

So, if you haven't been taking notes until now, God will forgive you, [*laughter*] but this would be a good time to begin because I'm going to be explaining to you three mistakes that Amos made— Did I say Amos? I meant Asaph. Three mistakes that Asaph made when he recognized he was on the brink of leaving the faith.

First of all, he said this, "I realized I've overestimated their prosperity." He says in verse 18, "Truly you set them in slippery places."

Wait a moment. What do you mean slippery places? That's how this psalm began, did it not? Did he not say, "You know, I almost slipped and fell"? But they're the ones that are in slippery places. "You make them fall to ruin. How they are destroyed in a moment, swept away utterly by terrors! Like a dream when one awakes, O Lord, when you rouse yourself, you despise them as phantoms."

Verse 22, "I was brutish and ignorant; I was like a beast before you." He's saying they may have this kind of prosperity, but it's not going to last. They're going to have to die, and it's all going to end. It's all coming to an end. He says, "I was like a beast." There is not a single cow in all of

Illinois who says to herself, "You know, I shouldn't eat too much because we're living in an inflationary era, and what I should do is make sure I have some food for tomorrow." No, just gobble it up. Gobble up everything you possibly can and don't worry about tomorrow. So, he says, "I was like a beast before you." He says, "These people are going to die and many of them are going to die unexpectedly."

Many years ago, in this church, there was a man (He could be here this morning. If he is, I'd like to shake his hand.) who's an expert in Chicago cemeteries. You know, this guy, who is perfectly normal in other ways, [*laughter*] when he has an extra afternoon, he goes to another cemetery. So, he'll show you all the Communists [who] are buried here, and [anyone else of interest] who's buried there. I don't know. We began on a Saturday morning and went all day until evening, from one cemetery to another, and it was fascinating.

One of the things you notice is the differentiation between gravestones. There are those whose names can no longer even be seen because they are small stones, and the weather has destroyed the stone. And then you come across one like Potter Palmer of the Palmer House, who helped rebuild Chicago after the [Great] Chicago Fire, and it's built like a Greek temple. It's unbelievable, with some very nice words.

By the way, I have to tell you this. Somebody said to

Palmer, "You know, when you die, your wife is going to remarry, and the man she marries, he's going to get all your money." And Palmer said, "If, when I die, my wife remarries and her husband gets all of my money, he is going to need it if he gets married to my wife." [*laughter*]

But the thing I noticed about all this is even though the gravestones are very different, there is a commonality in the cemetery. Everybody is dead. The statistics on death are very impressive.

One of the things I've noticed as I've watched the news is the number of people who die in their sixties and seventies. I've really been struck by that. I'll tell you, when I got into the eighties, I was so relieved. [*laughter*] I just said, "This is fantastic. I made it through the sixties and the seventies." [*applause*] So what he said is, "They may be rich, they may enjoy life, but it's not going to last. And it's not going to last very long, and they're going to be surprised because they are actually," he says, "walking as in a dream."

Just about two weeks ago, I came across a verse in Isaiah I'd never seen before. Isaiah 29. It says the wicked— they go to bed hungry. They're like a man who goes to bed hungry, dreams he is eating, and then he wakes up and he's hungry still; like a man who goes to sleep very thirsty, dreams he's having a nice cool drink, and wakes up thirsty still. [Asaph] says these people are like phantoms. They're sleepwalking. It's all going to be gone. They're living in an unreal reality. It's as if this going to last forever, but it's not. I overestimated their prosperity. "But then," he said, "I made another mistake and that is I underestimated my own prosperity."

Let's pick it up in [Psalm 73] verse 23: "Nevertheless, I am continually with thee: thou hast holden me by my right hand. Thou shalt guide me with thy counsel, and afterward receive me to glory. Whom have I in heaven but thee? and there is none upon the earth that I desire beside thee. My flesh and my heart faileth: but God is the strength of my heart, and my portion for ever."

He says, "I forgot I had God. I have His companionship here on Earth." "You guide me with thy counsel." (And I have to say about my life, I have seen the hand of God guide me in many wonderful ways.) "And then afterward, you receive me to glory." Wow. I'm a lot richer than I thought I was.

You know, there's nothing like having God. You know what the Bible says in Romans 8? "He that spared not his own Son, but delivered him up for us all, how shall he not with him also freely give us all things?"

Now, you know D.L. Moody was the founder of this church in 1864. Three years later, the Great Chicago Fire came. That's why the original building where the church was founded no longer exists. But Moody was able to escape. There's a famous story of him taking a picture with him, and they grabbed everything they could in the house and then they went to Des Plaines. Somebody said to him later, "So your house is destroyed, so you don't own anything." He said, "No, I'm really rich." "Oh." The guy probably thought, you know, "Do you have a stash of gold somewhere?" Moody took him to Revelation 21, where it says in the King James version, "He that overcometh shall inherit all things."

Did you know that as an heir of God, and a joint heir with Jesus Christ, that those who are redeemed are going to enter into an inheritance that is absolutely unbelievable? They will have an inheritance. [*applause*] You know, you say, "Oh, it's pie in the sky." Pie in the sky? Are you kidding? Ruling with Jesus Christ? "Those who overcome, I shall grant to sit with me on my throne, as I overcame and sat on my Father's throne." You're comparing that to pie? Not even pecan pie would compare with that. [*laughter*]

Imagine you are inheriting all things. And you remember when D.L. Moody died—before he died, he said those words, "Earth recedes, heaven opens. If this be death, it is glorious." Well.

Martin Lloyd Jones in England, before he died said to his family, "Don't pray for my healing. Don't rob me of glory." Don't rob me of glory. And Asaph is saying, "Oh, I forgot. I'm guided by the counsel of God." He says, "My flesh and my heart fails," which is certainly true of me when I watch the news. But he says, "My flesh and my heart fail, but God is the strength of my heart, and my portion forever." Wow.

There's a third mistake he made, and it's actually embedded in [Psalm 73] verse 21. The third mistake is, he says, "I judged God by how I felt, by my bitterness." He says, "I was embittered," and that's really the cause of many who deconstruct. You talk to them and you discover they are bitter because of their home life. I've had people say to me, "You know, I had a father who went to church. He seemed to be so religious, and everybody thought so highly of him. At home, he abused us. I hate my father. I hate his God. I'm out of here, thank you very much. I want nothing to do with Christianity. I deconstruct."

So, it could be the home life. It could be the church life. "You know the church, they wronged me, those meanies, those judgmental meanies. (And oftentimes what they say about us is true, unfortunately.) But because of the church, you know, I'm not going to have anything to do with that. Don't give me anything about this Christianity bit."

And then, the real biggie, and that is anger and bitterness toward God. And that, of course, is something that's understandable. We might say it's not excusable, but it is understandable.

Just last night, I was on a call-in program on about 200 stations, primarily stations in the south, and the host and I fielded questions for an hour. If you heard some of the things people told us about the abuse they endured, you'd understand why they struggled with God. You'd understand that. But God can handle it.

I want to tell you a true story about a woman. First of all, you have a mother who loves God, who serves God. She's married to a man. The man abuses the daughter. The daughter grows up. She wants nothing to do with her mother or her mother's God. The woman becomes famous. She makes tons of money, millions of dollars (and let's just look at this) and then she drives her car at a high speed into a building, and she is killed. She dies a few days later, with drugs and alcohol and the whole bit. Okay.

Now what we have to do is to take what I would suggest is a cost-benefit analysis, a cost-benefit analysis. How much did her rebellion cost her? It cost her the opportunity to get to know God, to walk with God. There's no evidence she ever received Christ as Savior, which means when she died—and the Bible says after death comes judgment—she was going to have to face God, alone, without a mediator, without Jesus who saves us from the wrath to come. She's going to have to face God alone. Terrifying.

That's what it cost her. Well, what was her benefit? Her benefit is she could wake up every single morning an angry woman. She could hold that bitterness in her heart and say, "I was abused. It's my mother's fault. It's her God's fault, and I'm going to live an alternate lifestyle. I'm going a different direction." And every day, she could wake up affirming the fact that she was filled with vengeance, but what a bad deal. What a bad deal.

When you and I find people who are deeply hurt, we have to be very, very sensitive. We have to enter into their pain. There are reasons why people are bitter. But we do have to help them to understand that bitterness keeps them from great blessing. And therefore it is so necessary for us— And I would say to all those of you who are listening, you've gone through a time of bitterness, no matter who it's about, and you hold it in your heart, and you say, "Well, until I get justice I'm not going to, you know, have anything to do with Christianity."

Well, we should do all that we can to bring about justice. Absolutely sure. But there's so many thousands of instances in this world where there will be no justice ever. You have to lay it down. You have to give it to God. You have to tell God what you think of Him. You have to be honest with Him, and you also have to realize He does promise that He heals the brokenhearted and binds up their wounds.

I want to say a word to those of you who are going through a period of doubt. You're asking questions. That's perfectly legitimate. You may be going through a time when you are having a crisis of faith. That is perfectly legitimate and understandable. God can handle it. Jesus can handle it.

Do you remember Matthew 11? John's in prison; John the Baptist is in prison and he begins to have doubts whether Jesus is the Messiah, of all things. This man who was the forerunner of Jesus, who saw all the miracles, he's beginning to say, "Oy vey, this doesn't make any sense at all, because it says in the Old Testament when Messiah comes, the doors of the prison are going to be opened. There's no doors opened here in my prison, thank you very much. If Jesus is the Messiah and has all this power, what in the world am I doing here?"

So, he sends a delegation to Jesus, and I'm sure it was said very kindly, but the delegation says this. "John wants to know, are you the one that we should look for, or should we look for someone else?"

And when they came to Jesus, Jesus didn't say, "I can't believe John had those doubts, after being together, we're at least half cousins, and now he's doubting if I'm the Messiah?" Jesus didn't say that. Jesus said, "Of those born of women, none is greater than John the Baptist."

If your doubts are honest doubts, God accepts you on that journey, and I suggest what you do is talk to leaders of the church, but also come to Jesus with your doubts. That's why I like the song so much:

Just as I am though tossed about,
With many a conflict, many a doubt.
Fightings within and fears without,

O Lamb of God I come, I come.

Come with your doubts.

To borrow a line, "Christianity is an anvil that has worn out many hammers." It can take your doubts. If you're an honest doubter. Pascal said this, and I'm paraphrasing, He said, "For those who seek the light, there's plenty of light; but for those who are committed to darkness, there's plenty of darkness to keep them blinded." So, are you an honest doubter? Are you open to belief? Then investigate Christianity. Look at the religion and see its history, yes, but also its tremendous compelling reasons to believe. And some of you need to take time out of your lives and have it out with God, so to speak, to lay it all before Him. Let Him know how you feel, and deal with your doubt, with your resentment, with your anger, because if you don't, you will be keeping yourself from blessings, many, many, many blessings.

There is a story which I've not been able to verify, but it certainly could be true because William Gladstone was the prime minister of England, who was a very dedicated Christian. The story is that a young man came to him and said, "I need some guidance." Gladstone said, "What do you plan to do?" The young man said, "Well, I'd like to get a good education." Gladstone said, "That's good, and what then?" He said, "Well, actually I'd like to be elected to

Parliament so I could do some good for the whole country of England." Gladstone said, "It's good to aim high. That's good, but what then?" The young man said, "Well, you know after that, I am thinking maybe in my old age I can write some books to help others and to help them learn lessons I've learned." Gladstone said, "That's good, but what then?" The young man said, "Well, I guess I'm going to have to die." Gladstone said, "That's right, and what then?" And the young man said, "I've really not given that much thought." And Gladstone said, "Young man, get on your knees and stay on your knees until you have thought life through to the very end."

Look at how this Psalm ends. Verse 27, "For behold, those who are far from you will perish; you put an end to everyone who is unfaithful to you. But for me (Praise God.) it is good to be near God; I have made the Lord God my refuge, that I might tell of all your works."

Two different paths when you see the long-range point of view.

I'm going to give you a sentence now, and after I give you that sentence, we're going to pray, and in this prayer—it is not a prayer in which you can make things right with God. That takes time, until you can really come before God and deal with Jesus Christ, who is the way to the Father to deal with God issues. But what you can do in that prayer is you can say, "God, with your help I will do anything to be fully right with you because I realize it is the end that matters."

Now, I'm going to give you a sentence that I want you to write down. I want you to laminate it. I want some of you who are creative to make some plaques you can hang up in your home. And it is one single sentence. Are you ready to write?

"The only thing that really matters is what matters forever."

Let's pray together.

Our Father, we are people who go through seasons of doubt. We are people who struggle with our faith. We're people who sometimes can't figure out where we're at.

I pray for everyone who's on a spiritual journey, even those who don't know exactly where they are on this journey. Help them, Father, to know it's the long-range point of view that matters.

We pray for those, Father, who need to spend time in your presence, to submit their bitterness and their anger and let it all spill out. Help them to know you can handle it. And help them to also know you do indeed bind up the brokenhearted and bind up their wounds. And may we always remember, Lord, that the only thing that really matters is what matters forever.

We ask in the blessed name of Jesus whom we love, Amen.

ERWIN W. LUTZER

STUDY GUIDE

Read Psalm 73:1–14

1. How would you define "deconstruction"? Why do you think many people deconstruct (have doubts about or even leave the Christian faith) today? (pp. 7, 17).

2. Deconstruction takes different forms (pp. 7, 17, 20). Why would someone intellectually or emotionally challenge the Christian faith?

3. Do you think people wrestling with doubt about God's goodness want more of Jesus as He truly is, or less? Why?

4. Asaph makes three mistakes which led him to doubt God's goodness. Which of the three do you relate to the most and why? (pp. 13, 15, 16)

Read Psalm 73:15–22

5. What does it mean to cause others to stumble? (p. 12). How could oversharing your doubts about Christianity on social media cause others to stumble? How can oversharing on social media be dangerous for your own soul?

6. If the community, culture, and institutions tasked with representing God don't do it well, then God Himself is often called into question. How can we avoid letting bitterness from a bad experience keep us from the blessing of knowing God? (pp. 16ff).

7. What's the difference between honest doubts and disbelief? What role does church history or reading the Bible play in strengthening our faith in God?

Read Psalm 73:22–28

8. How can we reconstruct our faith in God based on what's good, beautiful, and true? According to Psalm 73, what is the value of trusting God?

9. What's a biblical response to being hurt by Christians? What kind of relationships are important as we process hurtful or offensive experiences?

10. How do our riches in Christ remind us of who we are? How did God's sanctuary help Asaph to see heaven's perspective? (pp. 12, 20).

moodymedia.org/rebuilding

Share Pastor Lutzer's message with others.

Made in the USA
Monee, IL
04 March 2024

54143118R00022